DISCOVERING YOUR IOWA CIVIL WAR ANCESTRY

SECOND EDITION

BY STEVE MEYER

1993 All rights reserved.

This book, or any portion, may not be reproduced without permission.

COMMUNITY COLLEGE LRC
MARSHALLTOWN, IOWA 50158

Published by Meyer Publishing, Garrison, IA.

940410

ISBN No. 0-9630284-1-3

First edition printed August 1993
Second edition printed January 1994

DEDICATION

This book is dedicated to the memory of John Ridge, Job Brolliar, Elijah Hull, Thomas Patten, George Johnson, Robert Robertson, David Robertson, and James H. Willford, the long forgotten comerades from Carlisle Grove. And also the first two from the Garrison area to give their lives so that we may enjoy what we have today, Peter Kabrick and Samuel C. Martin, both of whom lived in the long forgotten community of Gomersal.

CONTENTS

INTRODUCTION	4
AN EXAMPLE: LONG FORGOTTEN COMRADES	6
WHAT IS YOUR OBJECTIVE?	19
DISCOVERING YOUR ANCESTORS AFFILIATION	20
FINDING OUT WHAT HE DID	
ARCHIVAL AND PRIMARY MATERIAL	25
BOOKS, MAGAZINES, AND OTHER SOURCES	32
A FEW OTHER HELPFUL HINTS AND SOURCES	39
ANOTHER EXAMPLE: FIRST REMINDERS OF A COSTLY WAR	41
APPENDIX A: STATE HISTORICAL INSTITUTIONS	49
APPENDIX B: IOWA CIVIL WAR REGIMENTAL HISTORY BOOKS	53
APPENDIX C: CIVIL WAR MAGAZINES AND JOURNALS	59
CIVIL WAR ANCESTOR NOTES	60

INTRODUCTION

Grandad always told me that Great Great Great Uncle Erastus served in the Civil War and fought in all the battles from Fort Sumpter to Appomattox. In the process he had six horses shot from under him, captured a whole regiment of rebel soldiers, and was twice left dead on a battle field. Did he? Or is this just a bunch of exaggerated folk lore? In such trivia passed from generation to generation lies our curiosity about family ties to that trying era of our nations past. Well, just what did Great Great Great Uncle Erastus do? Most likely he served in the armies of Grant and Sherman, endured agonizing marches, went for long periods of time with hardly a thing to eat, and may have participated in such noted battles as Pea Ridge, Fort Donnelson, Shiloh, Vicksburg, and Atlanta. It is possible that he served in the Army of the Potomac; some Iowans did. Maybe he was detailed West of the Mississippi River to fight indians. There is even the chance that he was among the less known, and rarely documented, souls who seen things differently and fought for the other side. Or, perhaps he did essentially nothing! The service record of some Iowa regiments was so mundane that they suffered few casualties and the troops were nearly bored to death of their volunteer military livelihood.

From 1861 to 1865 over 75,000 Iowans marched off to serve the Union cause in the Civil War. With that many Iowans serving so long ago, there are literally hundreds of thousands, probably even millions of descendants having ties to someone from Iowa who served in the Civil War. With some time, some patience, a little travel, a little investment, and a little inquisition, anyone can research their Iowa Civil War ancestors past, and uncover the true story of their heroic (sometimes less than heroic) service in our nations most trying time. Putting the story together consists of basically three steps:

1) Discovering your ancestors service affiliation

2) Finding out what his regiment did

3) Putting together your ancestors story.

Contained here are the where's and how's of doing just that. The only thing to remember before you begin your quest to discover your Iowa Civil War ties, and the drama of your ancestors service, is this is going to be an adventure So have fun!

AN EXAMPLE

To tantalize the ancestral researcher, I provide here the story revealed from one of my own civil war research exploits. The story of these eight Billy Yanks buried in an ancient pioneer cemetery gives an idea of how much a person can accomplish in piecing together events of a long forgotten Civil War soldiers life.

LONG FORGOTTEN COMRADES

I recall my first stroll through Carlisle Grove Cemetery as a high school lad. Determined to find a secret mushrooming spot in the woods just beyond, I took note of the monuments as I passed. An inscription on the side of the tallest one caught my attention: "David, Son of J. & J. Robertson, Died In Andersonville Prison July 22, 1864, Age 27 Yrs. 1 Mo. 7 Dys". Wow! I had listened in awe the year before as Bill Holland, a sharp old civil war buff, visited our American History Class and expounded on the Civil War and the horrors of Andersonville. I was absolutely in awe, right here before me was a memorial to a man who had walked the same soils as I, and had died while fighting to spare the unity of our great nation, in that place which made concentration camps look like church missions!

Founded by pioneer's, Carlisle Grove was one of the first cemeteries in Benton Counties Jackson Township. Neglected for years and over grown, the efforts of some thoughtful individuals had resurrected it a few years before my first inspiring visit. Nestled against a forest of mighty oaks, old obituaries mention a log church at the location, and to this day a wagon trail leading to the site is still faintly visible.

For some reason that discovery has always intrigued me. Twenty years later I am back at the memorial to David Robertson. Inspired by the recent Ken Burns television documentary on the Civil War, I find myself in the midst of writing what began as a book, but soon expanded to "books", on Iowa in the Civil War. For the writer, the researcher, inquisition reigns supreme. Who was David Robertson? What long forgotten story may lurk behind the inscription on his memorial? A quick walk across Carlisle Grove's one half acre of weathered and broken tombstones revealed others who had shared David Roberton's Civil War patriotism. Their graves are easily discernable from the rest. Star shaped bronze markers installed by members of the local GAR Post long ago, identify Carlisle Grove's Civil War veterans. I quickly find that John Ridge, Job Brolliar, Elijah Hull, Thomas Patten, and George Johnson had all seen military service in the epic era of the Civil War. The researchers mind broils, who were these men? What stories are buried with their bones six feet under?

To those of us whose inquiring minds cannot rest, an adventure rivaling that of any explorer awaits. The stories which unfolded in the researchers quest revealed heroism and struggles long forgotten in the singular event that challenged our great nation as never before and never since. My exploration began at the library. Old newspapers surely mention something, the researcher surmised. The first find, and perhaps the one which inspired more intensive research, was that of John Ridge. Seeing that Ridge's date of death was memorialized as October 1, 1864, perhaps he, like Robinson, was another war casualty, the researcher reasons. What a tragic casualty it must have been! Ridge's obituary from the Oct. 12, 1864 issue of the VINTON EAGLE reads:

Death of Lieut. John Ridge.

It is with feelings of deep regret that we announce the death of John Ridge, 1st Lieutenant of Company G., 13th Iowa Infantry. He died on the 4th instant at the Louisville Hospital of a wound suffered in the terrible battle in front of Atlanta on the 22d of July. His age was 30 years.

His body was interred in its burying-ground of Jackson Township, some six miles west of this place, on Sunday last, in the presence of the largest concourse of relatives and friends ever assembled on a funeral occasion in Benton County. The procession was nearly a mile in length, and numbered over fifty carriages of one kind or another.

At the place of biding, the funeral services, which were conducted by Rev. S. M. Lee, of this town, Col. Shane, commander of the regiment to which the deceased belonged, at the request of Mr. Lee, gave a brief, but glowing history of

Lieut. Ridges's military career. He paid the highest tribute of praise to his qualities as a soldier and as a man. He was indeed one of Nature's noblemen, high souled, brave, and generous to a fault. In his death the Company has lost a faithful officer--one who was a brother to the men of his command, anticipating and providing for their every want so far as it was in his power to do so--and his family has lost a kind and affectionate husband, father, son, brother. He is cut down in his prime, but the memory of his virtues will be long cherished by his surviving relatives, neighbors and aquaintances.

Intrigued, I ask myself, if Ridge was so valiant, how do I find out more about him and the others? My question leads me to discover ancient Benton County History Books, a six volume compilation written in the early 1900's entitled "Roster and Record of Iowa Soldiers in the War of the Rebellion," the massive 128 volume "Official Records of the Union and Confederate Armies in the War of the Rebellion," and numerous other musty old accounts, books, and reminisces of the Civil War. I also discover the wealth of information available on individual soldiers through the National Archives, and equally impressive archives at the State Historical Society of Iowa headquarters in Iowa City and Des Moines.

From the "Roster and Record of Iowa Soldiers" John Ridge's military career, his leadership ability as a soldier, and his success in the electorate system used for company officers of volunteer regiments during the Civil War is described:

> Ridge, John. Age 26. Residence Vinton, nativity Ohio. Enlisted Sept. 27, 1861 as First Corporal. Mustered Oct 28, 1861. Promoted Fifth Sergeant April 10, 1862; Fourth Sergeant April 30, 1862; Second Sergeant June 15, 1862; First Sergeant July 5, 1862; Second Lieutenant March 13, 1863; First Lieutenant April 29, 1863. Wounded in right side July 20, 1864, Atlanta, Ga. Died of wounds Oct. 4, 1864, Louisville, Ky.

On the very same page only a few listings below from the same regiment and company, the 13th Iowa Infantry Company G, I notice:

> Robertson, David. Age 26. Enlisted Jan. 2, 1864. Mustered Jan. 19, 1864. Missing in action and taken prisoner. Died while a prisoner of war Aug. 26, 1864, Andersonville, Ga. Buried in National Cemetery, Andersonville, Ga. Grave 6572

The researchers quest becomes even more interesting. Could there have been an association between Ridge and Robertson? What of the other "Boys in Blue" buried on that lonely hill top? As history records it, the 13th Iowa Infantry, Company G had its origins much the same as many other Iowa companies during the civil war -- locally. The nearly 100 members of Company G had all came from Benton County. No doubt, many who where chums before the war, marched off to war together. During the war, the 13th earned the nickname "Crockers Greyhounds" as a tribute to the regiments first Colonel Marcellus M. Crocker, and the regiments noted quickness on foot.

Now, I must find out, were any of the others at Carlisle Grove in the same company? Further research finds another:

> Brolliar, Job. Age 31. Residence Vinton, nativity, Ohio. Enlisted Sept. 27, 1861. Mustered Oct 28, 1861. Died of chronic diarrhea May 23, 1862.

Startling, three of the six known veterans at Carlisle Grove, all from the same regiment and company, all three war fatalities. One died from wounds, one was among "The Immortal Roll of 214 Loyal Sons of Iowa Who Died While Confined in Andersonville Prison," and one died the death most common among soldiers of that terrible war--disease.

Continuing the quest, the head stones of Elijah Hull and Thomas Patten bore their service affiliation, the 37th Iowa Infantry Co. A. From the "Roster and Record of Iowa Soldiers" I find:

> Hull, Elijah. Age 54. Residence Vinton, nativity Pennsylvania. Enlisted Sept. 16, 1862. Mustered Nov. 6, 1862. Discharged for disability May 18, 1864, Rock Island, Il.

Patten, Thomas. Age 52. Residency Muscatine. Enlisted Dec. 27, 1862. Mustered Feb. 28, 1863. Discharged for disability March 11, 1865, Gallipolis, Ohio.

These were older men, beyond the age of soldiering! The researcher pries deeper into Iowa's commitment to the Union cause, and finds they were members of Iowa's famous "Greybeard" regiment. In Iowa, a higher percentage of men within the acceptable age limits for volunteers served in the Civil War than any other state in the Union. So fervent was the desire of Iowans to serve that special permission was gained from the federal government to form a regiment of men beyond the acceptable age of 45. This was the 37th Iowa Infantry, the only regiment of its kind in the entire Union army. Enrolled in the 37th were fathers and even grand fathers of 1300 sons and grandsons already off to the war. The 37th was not too, and did not, see any active combat fighting except for a few skirmishes with bushwhackers. They were detailed to various guard and garrison duties. It was mundane, yet they performed vital functions of the war machine, and their service allowed younger men more fit for the ardors of combat to serve at the front.

Last, we have George Johnson. George came to Iowa following the Civil War. To find George's service record it was necessary to first find his obituary. From his obituary I discover George Johnson seen a different side of the war not seen by the other five who were part of General William Tecumseh Sherman's great Army of the Tennessee. George Johnson served in the 22d Pennsylvania Cavalry Co. J, part of the Army of West Virginia. George spent the war on horseback, a relegation not achieved as often as it was wanted by those who enlisted for service in the Civil War. Of the six known Civil War veterans at Carlisle Grove, George Johnson was the only one to see the end of the war without being disabled or giving the supreme sacrifice.

The researcher now knows the background of all six soldiers. Yet, inquisition is never satisfied until the last shovel of earth covering these long forgotten souls is turned. Perhaps somewhere some note worthy mention of these departed comrades could be found. I'm back to David Robertson. Knowing that century old Benton County history books contain family histories of the era, I air the musty pages of these ancient volumes. Immediately, I make an intriguing find. On the Robertson Family stone at Carlisle Grove, two other brothers are memorialized along with David: William who died on June 14, 1861 at age 21, and Robert who died in October 1870 at age 23. I find that family history records Robert as having served in the 9th Iowa Cavalry during the Civil War. In the same Benton County history book Robert Robertson receives no mention among the honor roles of Benton County Veterans, neither is he mentioned in the Carlisle Grove cemetery plot as a veteran. I verify Robert Robertson's service record in the "Roster and Record of Iowa Soldiers":

> Robertson, Robert. Age 18. Residence Toledo, nativity Illinois. Enlisted Oct 24, 1863. Mustered out Feb. 3, 1866, Little Rock, Ark.

Two things become obvious with this find. For one, the local record keeping systems of this bygone era allowed at least one veteran to be forgotten. And, by extrapolating Robert Robertson's age at death back to his age at enlistment, and comparing it to his age as listed in the "Roster and Record of Iowa Soldiers," we find he did something not uncommon, lied about his age so he could get into the military. As the war ground into its later years, recruitment officers compensated for recruiting difficulties by not even questioning willing volunteers such as the under aged Robert Robertson. Lost to time are the feelings of his parents over their teen age enlistee.

Now, the researcher asks, if there was one forgotten, could there be others? Amongst the 90 stones at Carlisle Grove are others who died during the Civil War years, perhaps some other hapless souls never received their due recognition. William Robertson is the first likely candidate for investigation. Fortunately, an obituary was found which confirmed his death as something comparable to a modern day automobile accident, he was kicked in the head by a horse. It must have been a tragic decade for J & J Robertson. From their family of seven, three sons were cut down in their prime: David, Robert and William. William had a twin, Andrew. Andrew is not buried at Carlisle Grove, but he did enlist in Iowa's last three year regiment, the 40th Iowa Infantry, and did survive the war.

The search continues. I noted a dozen entries into the little cemetery during the Civil War that could have been veterans. Painstakingly I eliminate each one after thorough research, until I reach the last, James H. Willford, memorialized at Carlisle Grove as dying in June, 1863 at an age of 21 years. From the Benton County history book I find a James H. Willford in the 28th Iowa Infantry, Co. D. Checking the "Roster and Record of Iowa Soldiers," I find:

> Willford, James H. Residency Vinton, nativity, Ohio. Enlisted Aug. 1, 1862. Mustered Sept. 4, 1862. Wounded May 16, 1863, Champion Hills, Miss. Died of wounds, May 29, 1863, Bakers Creek, Miss.

Seeing some discrepancy in the dates I confirm from the Willford family history that J. P. Willford (shown as James H. Willfords father on the family stone) did loose a son in the Civil War. As the dates show, grave markers can be in error also. The researcher finds a second forgotten veteran at Carlisle Grove.

The last shovel is not yet turned. From the National Archives, actual war time records including muster roles, personal descriptions, surgeons reports, disability reports, personal correspondences, and pension records are secured for all of Carlisle Grove's veterans. Some of these records lay in files which may have been unopened for 130 years. By cross referencing this data with regimental history information, the whole story of these gallant souls comes to life.

John Ridge and Job Brolliar went into the service together. Records show that Brolliar was soon afflicted with his malady and spent a good share of his time in the hospital. He was able to participate in one great battle, Pittsburg Landing (Shiloh) along with Ridge on April 6 & 7, 1862. April 6 was the day General Grant was caught by surprise and thousands of green Iowa troops who had yet to experience combat (Ridge and Brolliar among them) were hurled into the bloody struggle. Of Grant's 39,000 troops on that day, 6,600 (11 regiments) were Iowans. It was a day when Iowa troops saved the Union Army in the west, keeping Confederate forces at bay in a place referred to by Confederates as "The Hornets Nest" while Grant regrouped with reinforcements, allowing him to recapture lost ground the following day. In the two days of this great battle, Union losses were 11,000 with the 13th infantry suffering 24 dead, 139 wounded and 9 missing. Ridge received his first promotion two days later. A few months later Brolliar was sent home where he died from his infirmity. Carlisle Grove's first reminder of war's realism left a wife and three children aged 4 to 8.

The next visitation of honor at Carlisle Grove would be that of James H. Willford. The 28th Iowa Infantry had amongst its ranks two companies of Benton Countians, Company's A & D. On the 16th of March, 1863 at a key battle in General Grant's Vicksburg Campaign the 28th Iowa found themselves in the thick of it at the Battle of Champion Hills. Grant's 29,000 Union troops were pitted against Confederate General John Pemberton's 20,000 rebels in a see-saw battle. Some positions on the battle field changed hands several times as charges and counter charges were made by each side. It ended in a Union victory at a cost of 410 dead, 1844 wounded and 167 missing. Confederate casualties were 381 killed, 1800 wounded and 1670 missing. The 28th Iowa Infantry engaged the enemy at a location known as Champion's Hill. Brigadier General Alvin P. Hovey, commander of the 12th Division of which the 28th was a part reported:

> "I cannot think of this bloody hill without sadness and pride. Sadness for the great loss of my true and gallant men; pride for the heroic bravery they displayed. No prouder division ever met as vastly superior foe and fought with more unflinching firmness and stubborn valor. It was, after the conflict, literally the hill of death; men, horses, cannon, and the debris of an army lay scattered in wild confusion. Hundreds of the Twelfth Division were cold in death or writhing in pain...
>
> I never saw fighting like this. The loss of my division, on this field alone, was nearly one third of my forces engaged. Of the Twenty-ninth Wisconsin, Twenty-fourth and Twenty-eighth Iowa, in what words of praise shall I speak? Not more than six months in the service, their record will compare with the oldest and best tried regiments in the field..."

Colonel James R. Slack who commanded a brigade consisting of the 24th and 28th Iowa, 47th Indiana, 56th Ohio, and the 1st

Missouri Battery described opening moments of the struggle at Champion's Hill:

> "Then the battle began with great fury, our troops advancing for the purpose of driving the enemy from the cover of the woods, which was done at double-quick and in a most gallant manner, the men loading and firing as they advanced, and unfalteringly recieved a most deadly fire from the enemy; yet they pressed forward, as men only can do who are prompted by intelligent motives of patriotic devotion to a common country, until the rebel force was driven from the covering and forced to fall back a distance of 200 yards, with terrible loss, the ground being literally covered with dead and wounded rebels..."

Casualties amongst the ranks of Benton County "Boys in Blue" in the 28th Iowa Infantry were ten percent. Among them was James H. Willford who died from his wounds two weeks later. He had not yet married and left no children. His death would be amongst the many suffered by his parents. Of their 13 children only 3 were alive when the father, Jacob Willford, died in 1891.

In 1863 Robert Robertson's lie achieved his goal and here he was, 16 years old, entering the mans world of the military. Unfortunately, his regiment had a rather lack luster service record. The 9th Iowa Cavalry was stationed in areas of Tennessee, Arkansas, and Missouri where the war had essentially expired itself. Soldiers of the 9th who bided their time in the military performed various guard duties and chased confederate raiders such as the infamous Quantrill. The regiment never participated in a single battle, the only action its members experienced was some skirmishing. Robert Robertson's tenure in the 9th Iowa may have proved frustrating to such a young lad, no doubt full of vigor and hot for the fight.

The lack luster service of the 9th Iowa Cavalry is surpassed by the 37th Iowa Infantry in which Elijah Hull and Thomas Patten served. Knowing you would be sequestered to nothing but guard and garrison duty must have been a deterrent, yet the 37th had no problem filling its roster, and they all served honorably. Of the 1041 soldiers enrolled in the 37th Iowa only 3 were killed and 4 wounded. National Archive records reveal Elijah Hull as one of the wounded. How he was wounded is lost to time. It could have been at the hands of the enemy, or it could have been at the wrong end of a comrades misfired gun. We also find from National Archives records that Hull's fellow member Thomas Patten had some questionable occurrences in his service record. He is shown as enlisting at an earlier date, but refusing to muster in. He obviously had a change of heart later. The records also show Patten as "Due U.S. by sentence of Court Martial $5.00" in 1864. He must have gotten into trouble for something, exactly what is unknown, but $5.00 was not pocket change in those days!

    The most epic story of Carlisle Grove is that of Lieut. John Ridge and David Robertson. As the war ground on, the ranks of many Iowa Regiments became depleted due to war casualties and expiration of service terms. To replenish regiments, the government had instituted various financial incentives for volunteers called bounties and premiums. Recruiting parties from the regiments, which consisted of an officer or two and a couple of privates, were dispatched back to the area of their companies origin to solicit new members. From November of 1863 to February 1864 the gallant Lieut. Ridge was back home on such a mission. Back to the front in March, Ridge and the replenished 13th Iowa Infantry became part of the massive 98,000 man army which assaulted the Confederate stronghold Atlanta, Ga. in June. The Atlanta campaign dragged on for four months. On July 20-22, Confederate General John Bell Hood went on the offensive in heavy fighting referred to as the Battle of Atlanta. Rebel soldiers left their entrenchments and came after Sherman's army. It ended in a route for the Union army which inflicted casualties of 8000 dead, wounded, and missing upon the confederates. Union casualties were 430 killed, 1559, wounded and 1733 missing.

    The Union's triumph over Hood set in motion the fall of Atlanta on Sept. 1, and a strategic victory in the Confederacies fate. Though a great victory for General Sherman, he grieved. His "right hand man" General James Birdseye McPherson was killed in the battle. While Sherman grieved, Benton County grieved. The 13th Iowa Infantry bore the brunt of the battle. Losses to the 13th from July 20-22 were an astounding 52 percent. Colonel John Shane of the 13th Iowa Infantry who commanded the Third Brigade during the Battle of Atlanta wrote daily reports of the action. On the 21st he wrote:

"The loss to the brigade during the action, which did not last more than thirty minutes, was severe, principally falling on the Thirteenth, Fifteenth, and Sixteenth Regiments Iowa Infantry...

I cannot speak in too high terms of praise of the conduct of both officers and men in the brigade during the brief but bloody conflict. The advanced line was particularly exposed to a terrible fire of grape, canister, and musketry from the moment the movement commenced. The Thirteenth Iowa in that brief space of time lost one-fourth its men.but although thus suffering and their comrades being momentarily cut down, every man acted the hero and veteran that he was, until the eminence had gained and secured from danger of being retaken..."

Of action engaged in by the 13th Iowa on the 22nd Shane wrote:

"Two companies (A and G) detached in the beginning of the contest and posted on the right of the Eleventh Iowa,....I regret to say, that from all the information I have been enabled to obtain in regard to them, I am reluctantly led to the conclusion that about three-fourths of the men composing those companies were, whilst supporting and bravely fighting side by side with the men of the Eleventh and Sixteenth Regiments Iowa Infantry, killed or captured, including all the commissioned officers on duty with them at the time."

During the 21st and 22nd Company G suffered 11 killed, 24 wounded, 7 captured, and 2 missing; 44 out of 100 men in the company. Of the 24 wounded four would later die, including Lieut. Ridge who died three months later in an officers hospital at Louisville, KY. From military records it appears his wife Jane was by his side. Ridge had participated in many of the notable battles of Grant and Sherman. Among them were Shiloh, Corinth, Port Gibson, Raymond, Champion Hills, Big Black River, Kennesaw Mountain, and Nickajack Creek. In addition to his wife he left a young daughter.

Whether David Robertson participated in any battles before the Battle of Atlanta is unclear. He is shown as sick and in the hospital in January and June of 1864. Entering the Battle of Atlanta, probably still ailing, he was captured on July 22 and sent to Andersonville prison.

For even the most fit, Andersonville was a struggle for survival. Robertson probably entered Andersonville less than healthy, and he lasted only one month. Daily they buried the emaciated dead by the hundred in trenches at Andersonville. A captured Private, Dorance Atwater of the 2nd New York Cavalry, because of his gifted penmanship, was in charge of the books in which prisoner deaths were recorded. In August 1864 he began to secretly make a copy of the list which he smuggled out when he was exchanged in March of 1865. Were it not for Atwater the trenches would be nameless mass graves. Grave 6572 in the Andersonville National Cemetery is that of David Robertson. Two others from company G, Lewis Lord and William Merchant would perish in Andersonville also. David Robertson left a wife, but no children. His wife Margaret no doubt found the $60.00 bounty and $2.00 premium he was paid at the time of his enlistment useful. From David Robertson's records we find he was was recruited by Lieut. John Ridge. They both went down in the same battle.

While the Benton County Boys tramped around the South with Sherman and Grant, George Johnson spent his time in the battle infested areas of Virginia, Pennsylvania, and Maryland. Scouting and skirmishing activities were the main activity for Johnson's company. Of all the battles which occurred in this area, the only one the 22nd Pennsylvania Cavalry is mentioned as directly participating in was the Battle of Opequon Creek (Winchester) on September 19, 1864. His cavalry unit was very active, however in many of the perimeter activities that went on with numerous other battles. He exited the war a Sergeant, came to Benton County to visit relatives, liked Benton County, relocated to Jackson Township, and became a successful farmer.

As I dwelled through accounts and histories of the individual soldiers, a relationship developed that spanned over a century of time. Visions of battlefield action came to life, long silenced cannon roared again, and the tribulation of a most terrifying warfare, moved me to feel both military and pioneer hardships long forgotten. All eight of these men at Carlisle Grove listed farming as an occupation. They left the security of their fields for the battle fields. Four of the men never returned to till the soil again. Two returned with injuries and two escaped the war unscathed.

Iowa is dotted with cemeteries of all sizes, many of pioneer origin just like Carlisle Grove. Scarcely a cemetery will be found that is without Civil War veterans. Each has its own stories lurking beneath their weathered headstones. To those who seek, there in lie unrivaled stories of our countries most epic struggle, and the heroic part that those who trod the same ground as we, played in preserving what we have today.

WHAT IS YOUR OBJECTIVE?

Before you begin your search, you need to first determine what it is that you want to do. If all you want to do is find out if your ancestor is indeed a Civil War veteran, and also the unit he served in, your search may be easy. The chapter "DISCOVERING YOUR CIVIL WAR ANCESTORS AFFILIATION" should give you all of the help you need to obtain such information. The same principles can be applied even if you are researching a Civil War ancestor from another state.

If you want a more complete, detailed, depiction of your Civil War ancestors service commitment (something similar to "LONG FORGOTTEN COMRADES"), it is going to take a little more effort. The help you need in this adventure is found in the chapter "FINDING OUT WHAT HE DID." This portion of the search can be the most thrilling. As you research the history of Great Great Great Uncle Erastus' military unit, don't be surprised if you feel yourself filling his boots. Writings from the Civil War era, which you will be reading a lot of in an extensive search, are of a most graphic and poignant literary style. They become even more interesting to read when you have a tie, a family tie, to them. If you already have information concerning your ancestors service affiliation, you may want to skip the first step, "DISCOVERING YOUR CIVIL WAR ANCESTORS AFFILIATION," and move right on to the fun part, "FINDING OUT WHAT HE DID."

DISCOVERING YOUR ANCESTORS AFFILIATION

One piece of information that everything hinges on in putting together your Civil War ancestors story is their affiliation; the branch of service, regiment, and company, (assuming you know your ancestors name) that your ancestor served in. Without this vital information you are going to be "lost at sea." A variety of sources can be tapped to help you find this information.

To find your ancestors affiliation first try researching any previous family history. Family histories often document an ancestors service affiliation. If you don't have such a document prepared by some thoughtful past family genealogist, try looking in a County History book. Over the years following the Civil War, every county in Iowa (at least I'm not aware of any that haven't) has had its history printed at least once, and most likely several times. First determine what county your ancestor lived in at his time of enlistment, then get a county history book from that county. Get the oldest issue you can, the one closest in its printing to the years of the Civil War, 1861 - 1865. County history books printed directly following the Civil War and up to the early 1900's included rosters of those who served from the county and often a sentence or two about what they did. You will find in a county history book scores of names listed as serving in a particular regiment and company. During the war, companies to fill the regiments were often recruited locally. You may have to comb the rosters and take it on a name by name basis to find you're ancestor. County histories also contained stories of local interest about particular soldiers and/or local companies.

If your search of county records proves fruitless, don't give up. Recorded rosters in county history books are sometimes incomplete, neglecting to mention some veterans, and it is possible your ancestor served in a company that was mustered out of a neighboring county, or perhaps even another state. Such incidents happened often, as men crossed county lines, even state lines to join other companies either because of previous associations or an inability to get into a locally raised company. Hence, you may find your ancestor listed among the roster of a neighboring counties veterans. In just a few more paragraphs we'll talk about finding those who enlisted in regiments from other states.

Most old county history books also contain biographical information of many of its citizens and families. Be certain to check these dissertations also, for usually recorded is the service affiliation of any family members who served in the Civil War.

Cemeteries and obituaries are another good local source for discovering your Civil War ancestry. Some headstones of veterans note the service affiliation of those buried beneath. Many do not. If the tombstone is marked with the bronze star bearing the initials G.A.R. (Grand Army of the Republic) as most, but not all, Civil War veteran graves are, the soul beneath did indeed serve. However, as noted in the "LONG FORGOTTEN COMRADES" story, due to the fragmented record keeping of the era, there are numerous instances of veterans never receiving the bronze marker they so nobly earned. Markers were erected by local G.A.R. posts following the war or later by American Legion posts. The passage of time and vandalism is another cause to missing or misplaced markers also. If you can locate an obituary of the veteran you are researching, their service affiliation is usually noted. For casualties during the war, it is not uncommon for mention of the soldiers death to not occur for several weeks following the incident. So, when you are searching old newspapers, if you do not discover anything within the first week following a death, continue searching forward. While perusing the papers, investigate war correspondence and battle casualty reports also. They usually were written by someone with local connections who mentioned local losses and the activities of locally recruited companies. Old newspapers and microfilmed copies of old newspapers are maintained by newspaper publishers themselves, local libraries, sometimes local historical societies, and sometimes the local courthouse. Additionally, a good stock of many newspapers can be found at the State Historical Society of Iowa locations in Des Moines and Iowa City.

Old G.A.R. post records may help. Numerous G.A.R. posts were formed in Iowa following the war, and in their records may be found the service affiliation of their members. As time went on and Civil War veterans died, the posts vanished. Some of their records were retained by local American Legion or American Veterans associations and some were turned over to local historical societies. The State Historical

Society of Iowa in Des Moines has records of the locations of various G.A.R. posts and has in its archives many records and rosters of these organizations.

Precise confirmation of your Civil War ancestor, provided he was from an Iowa volunteer regiment, can be obtained from the compilation "ROSTER AND RECORD OF IOWA SOLDIERS IN THE WAR OF THE REBELLION" that was published in the early 1900's. Most libraries, some local historical societies, and both of the State Historical Society of Iowa locations in Des Moines and Iowa City have copies of the "ROSTER AND RECORD." For volunteers who joined Iowa regiments the "ROSTER AND RECORD" is complete. Contained in the six volumes are regimental information as follows:

> Volume I - 1st - 8th Infantry Regiments
> Volume II - 9th - 16th Infantry Regiments
> Volume III - 17th - 31st Infantry Regiments
> Volume IV - 1st - 9th Cavalry Regiments
> Volume V - 31st - 48th Infantry Regiments, 1st Regiment
>   African Infantry, 1st - 4th Batteries Light Artillery
> Volume VI - Miscellaneous Civil War, plus Mexican War,
>   Indian Campaigns, Spanish American, and Phillippine Wars.

You will find a brief outline of the service record of every volunteer veteran of the Civil War in the "ROSTER AND RECORD." Also included are a few pages of regimental history information. If all you know is the regiment your ancestor served in, you can use this reference to find his service record, but you are going to have to do a little sifting. If your veteran is not mentioned anywhere in Volumes I - V of the "ROSTER AND RECORD" either he did not serve at all in the Civil War, or he served in an out of state or Regular Army regiment. Several thousand Iowans served in companies derived from another state, particularly the border states (in particular Missouri), and there were hundreds who served in the Regular Army.

To identify a soldier who served in an out of state or regular Army regiment, first look in Volume VI of the "ROSTER AND RECORD." Here again, you may have to do some sifting, particularly if all you know is the state your ancestor served from. If you do not find your veteran mentioned here, do not be discouraged, the "ROSTER AND RECORD" is very incomplete in the areas of out of state enlistees and regular army enlistees. Iowa did not receive all of the records of out of state enlistees, and soldiers who served in the regular army did not receive the attention given volunteer forces, mostly because it was "their job." Also in Volume VI, concerning the Civil War, are recorded some of those who served in the Navy and the Mississippi Marine Brigade. But, once again, these two areas are incomplete. Only a handful of Iowans are mentioned as serving in the Navy during the Civil War, though several hundred Iowans actually served in the Navy. The problem of not being recorded is due to Iowa having no Naval recruiting offices, forcing Iowans wishing to serve in the Navy to travel out of state to enlist. Those who entered the Mississippi Marine Brigade usually did so by transfer from the volunteer regiments, for which the information never found its way into the "ROSTER AND RECORD." Also identified in Volume VI are those who served in the Northern and Southern Border Brigades, The Engineers Regiment of the West, and some enlistments not connected with the Civil War.

Your final assault in identifying the service records of a Civil War veteran who served in either an out of state regiment, the regular army, the Navy, or the Mississippi Marine brigade is either National Archive records (see the next chapter) or the historical society of the state from which your veteran served. Most states have some sort of compilation similar to the "ROSTER AND RECORD." A listing of the various state agencies responsible for Civil War records is found in Appendix A. Historians at these agencies are generally good about helping. They will not research just a name, but must have a regiment, or at least a clue to a regiment, to reference in conducting the search for you.

If after all of this effort you are still unable to come up with the information you need, your last ditch effort may be the services of a professional researcher. The author of this guidebook conducts such research, and the State Historical Society of Iowa maintains a list of professional genealogy researchers who are qualified. In addition, if you are researching an ancestor who served in an out of state regiment, the various state historical organizations listed in Appendix A usually maintain a list of professional researchers who can help you. For the time and expense you may have involved in traveling to the state yourself to conduct research, having a professional assist you could very well be your easiest route.

FINDING OUT WHAT HE DID

Once you have the critical piece of information describing your ancestors affiliation you may be satisfied to stop there. Most people, however, will not. Its great fun to actually piece together just what Great Great Great Uncle Erastus did during the Civil War. It's possible to find out what battles he fought in, where his unit served, circumstances surrounding his death or discharge, and much more. You will have to use a variety of resources, but by the time you have completed your research you will find you can probably write what amounts to a small book on your ancestors involvement in the Civil War.

Archival and Primary Material

Your first inquiry should be to the National Archives in Washington D.C. The first step is requesting copies of the NATF Form 80 by writing to:

>National Archives
>And Records Administration (NNRG)
>7th and Pennsylvania Avenue N.W.
>Washington, D.C. 20408

An NATF Form 80 is required for all veteran research inquiries at the National Archives. A copy of the form is shown on pages 30 - 31. Fill the form out as completely as possible, providing as a minimum, the soldiers name, regiment, company, and such information as birth and death dates for sections 3, 5, 8, and 9. Without this information your search will be fruitless. Be sure to indicate in the upper left hand corner whether you are searching military or pension records. You cannot request both on the same inquiry. If you wish to receive both military and pension records you need to complete a separate form for both. Pension records are sometimes valuable for genealogical information as they indicate the immediate family, wife, children, and sometimes the parents of the soldier. They also indicate the manner and place of death. In a soldiers military records you may find his muster in roll, a descriptive roll, muster rolls that were taken periodically, muster out roll, casualty report(s), medical reports, prisoner of war reports, discharge papers, perhaps some promotional papers, and if you are lucky some personal correspondences. Some of these items may be missing, but generally, it has been my experience, that for the Iowa Volunteer Regiments the records are quite complete. For regulars its hit and miss, you may receive very complete records, or next to nothing at all, and in the case of Confederates, maybe nothing at all. When the latter is the case, you may wish to try the archives of the state the Confederate veteran served from (see Appendix A). If the ancestor you are researching was court martialed there should be a number somewhere in the National Archives file indicating a case number or court docket. The complete court martial proceedings can be obtained by writing back to the National Archives and giving them the case number.

How quickly you receive your information from the National Archives depends upon how busy the researchers are. Pension records take a little longer, but the normal turn around time is about one month. Cost for a search is $10.00 but can run more if there happens to be a lot of papers in a particular soldiers file. You can either pay for the search once they have confirmed back to you that they have located files concerning your ancestor, or you can pay by giving a credit card number along with the application. I prefer the credit card route, as this is the quickest. Be certain when filling out your request for information to do so in ink and to press hard, you are making four copies. Keep the last (pink) copy for yourself and send the completed form on to the address listed on the pink sheet. One additional tip on your request, be certain to print across the top of the form in bold letters SEND ALL RECORDS. If you do not, and there is anything extra in a soldiers file such as personal correspondence, physicians reports, etc., all you will receive are the muster roles, descriptive role, and discharge papers for the individual soldier.

If you require some special assistance or advice, you may either correspond or telephone the National Archives and talk to one of the Civil War researchers. My experience has been that they are very helpful. Even if you telephone them, and you are requesting more information of some specific type, they will still request that you mail a formal written request for information back to them including the NATF Form

80. The phone number for the Civil War section of the Military Reference Branch is: 202-501-5390. General information about the National Archives and the complete services of the administration can be recieved by calling 202-501-5402.

The National Archives also has three books available which will assist serious researchers. Two books, "THE UNION: A GUIDE TO FEDERAL ARCHIVES RELATING TO THE CIVIL WAR" by Munden and Beers, and "THE CONFEDERACY: A GUIDE TO THE ARCHIVES OF THE GOVERNMENT OF THE CONFEDERATE STATES OF AMERICA" by Henry Putney Beers, describe the locations of record groups and files at the National Archives containing information on a myriad of subjects pertaining to the Civil War. A third book, "A GUIDE TO CIVIL WAR MAPS IN THE NATIONAL ARCHIVES" is a general guide to over 8,000 maps relating to the Civil War in the Cartographic and Architectural Branch of the National Archives. All three can be purchased by calling the National Archives toll-free number 1-800-788-6282.

Next stop in your research is the State Historical Society of Iowa archives. You may be fortunate enough to find useful information in either of the archives. The addresses and phone numbers of each are: State Historical Society of Iowa, Capitol Complex, Des Moines, IA. 50319, ph. 515-281-5111; and State Historical Society of Iowa, 402 Iowa Avenue, Iowa City, Iowa, 52240, ph. 319-335-3916.

Both of our state archives have numerous holdings of what is referred to as primary material (diaries, letters, papers, reports, personal papers, and photos) from Iowa Civil War Soldiers. Who knows, your long gone ancestor may have left something that is housed in these collections, but don't get your hopes too high. What you may be more certain of finding is something written by another member of your ancestors regiment or company. This information is sometimes very helpful and usually very interesting depending upon how well the writer recorded information about the events of his service. Diaries in particular run the full gamut of everything from thorough details of everything that occurred in the soldiers life to diaries that record little more than the weather and how far they marched that day. If you find written material from another soldier in your ancestors company or regiment it is good reference data about

940410

significant events in the unit, and you may even find mention of your ancestor in such writings. Archival information at both of the locations is not duplicated in the holdings of the other. So, if you go to one location and find nothing, try the other!

All of the State Historical Society of Iowa staff are most helpful, and they can make photo copies of most any information you desire. To find out if there is anything from your ancestor or related to your ancestor in the archives, you will need to reference the card catalog in the Archives on the second floor at Iowa City. In Des Moines they have a very handy reference book which describes all of the Civil War holdings of the Des Moines archives. Additionally, at the Des Moines location, all of the records of the State of Iowa Adjutant General for the Civil War are housed. Various information is found in these reports including enlistment reports, camp reports, casualty reports, some battle reports, and numerous other bits of information. For each regiment the Adjutant General Records include two to three boxes of material. There is a great deal of corespondence in these records, and probably the answers to many questions about Iowan's in the Civil War. While you are at either location, you may wish to take a look at the books maintained in the general reference section. They both have many of the useful regimental history books and other books discussed later in this section.

If you happen to be dealing with a soldier who served in an out of state regiment, the historical organizations in each state (Appendix A) which serve the comparable function of the State Historical Society of Iowa, all maintain similar information as that found in the Iowa archives.

One other institution which maintains useful information is the U. S. Army Military History Institute at the Carlisle Army Barracks, Bldg. 22, Carlisle, PA. 17013-5008. ph. 717-245-3611. Like the State Historical Society of Iowa, the institute has diaries, papers, letters, and photos from Iowa Civil War soldiers in addition too regimental history information from numerous sources and practically anything that has been written in periodicals concerning specific regiments. Once again, the staff at Carlisle Army Barracks are most helpful, and for a fee will photocopy any documents or information you desire. Call them first, and they will send you a complete listing of their various holdings pertaining to a particular regiment.

Privately held collections, the collections of university libraries and county historical societies are other sources for primary material. Some have nothing, some may have a few letters or diaries (often from someone local if its a county society), and some of the university libraries have extensive collections. The only way to find out what is available is to ask. Privately held materials may be in the hands of collectors or someone who had the foresight to save all of the letters and the diary that Great Great Great uncle Erastus sent home from the war over 100 years ago. It might be buried in someones attic, but if you do find something that someone from your long lost relatives unit wrote, you've got a real find! You usually find these items by talking to some local historian. That local historian usually knows someone, who knows someone, who knows someone, but such is the trail of the researcher!

ORDER FOR COPIES OF VETERANS RECORDS

(See Instructions page before completing this form)

DATE RECEIVED IN NNRG

INDICATE BELOW THE TYPE OF FILE DESIRED AND THE METHOD OF PAYMENT PREFERRED.

1. FILE TO BE SEARCHED *(Check one box only)*
- ☐ PENSION
- ☐ BOUNTY-LAND WARRANT APPLICATION *(Service before 1856 only)*
- ☐ MILITARY

2. PAYMENT METHOD *(Check one box only)*
- ☐ CREDIT CARD *(VISA or MasterCard) for IMMEDIATE SHIPMENT of copies*
  - Account Number: _____ Exp. Date: _____
  - Signature: _____ Daytime Phone: _____
- ☐ **BILL ME** *(No Credit Card)*

REQUIRED MINIMUM IDENTIFICATION OF VETERAN - MUST BE COMPLETED OR YOUR ORDER CANNOT BE SERVICED

3. VETERAN *(Give last, first, and middle names)*	4. BRANCH OF SERVICE IN WHICH HE SERVED ☐ ARMY ☐ NAVY ☐ MARINE CORPS
5. STATE FROM WHICH HE SERVED	6. WAR IN WHICH, OR DATES BETWEEN WHICH, HE SERVED	7. IF SERVICE WAS CIVIL WAR, ☐ UNION ☐ CONFEDERATE

PLEASE PROVIDE THE FOLLOWING ADDITIONAL INFORMATION, IF KNOWN

8. UNIT IN WHICH HE SERVED *(Name of regiment or number, company, etc, name of ship)*	9. IF SERVICE WAS ARMY, ARM IN WHICH HE SERVED ☐ INFANTRY ☐ CAVALRY ☐ ARTILLERY *If other, specify:*
	Rank ☐ OFFICER ☐ ENLISTED	10. KIND OF SERVICE ☐ VOLUNTEERS ☐ REGULARS
11. PENSION/BOUNTY-LAND FILE NO.	12. IF VETERAN LIVED IN A HOME FOR SOLDIERS, GIVE LOCATION *(City and State)*	13. PLACE(S) VETERAN LIVED AFTER SERVICE
14. DATE OF BIRTH	15. PLACE OF BIRTH *(City, County, State, etc.)*	18. NAME OF WIDOW OR OTHER CLAIMANT
16. DATE OF DEATH	17. PLACE OF DEATH *(City, County, State, etc.)*	

NATIONAL ARCHIVES TRUST FUND BOARD   NATF Form 80 (rev. 4-92)

DO NOT WRITE BELOW - SPACE IS FOR OUR REPLY TO YOU

☐ NO -- We were unable to locate the file you requested above. **No payment is required.**

DATE SEARCHED	SEARCHER

☐ REQUIRED MINIMUM IDENTIFICATION OF VETERAN WAS NOT PROVIDED. Please complete blocks 3 (give full name), 4, 5, 6, and 7 and resubmit your order.

☐ A SEARCH WAS MADE BUT THE FILE YOU REQUESTED ABOVE WAS NOT FOUND. When we do not find a record for a veteran, this does not mean that he did not serve. You may be able to obtain information about him from the archives of the State from which he served.

☐ See attached forms, leaflets, or information sheets.

☐ ... -- We located the file you requested above. have made copies from the file for you. The cost for these copies is $10.

DATE SEARCHED	SEARCHER
FILE DESIGNATION	

Make your check or money order payable to NATIONAL ARCHIVES TRUST FUND. Do not send cash. Return this form and your payment in the enclosed envelope to:

NATIONAL ARCHIVES TRUST FUND
P.O. BOX 100221
ATLANTA, GA 30384-0221

PLEASE NOTE: We will hold these copies awaiting receipt of payment for only 45 days from the date completed, which is stamped below. After that time, you must submit another form to obtain photocopies of the file.

A74233

THIS IS YOUR MAILING LABEL	**NAME (Last, First, MI)**	
	STREET	
PRESS FIRMLY.	CITY, STATE	ZIP CODE

INVOICE/REPLY COPY - DO NOT DETACH

Books, Magazines and Other Sources

No event in American History has received as much attention as the Civil War. There are thousands of books on the subject, several magazines devoted to its study, and countless other writings about the Civil War published in various historical publications. In many of these publications lie information about Iowa in general during the Civil War, and more specific information concerning Iowa regiments and instances involving Iowans in the Civil War.

One starting place for collecting information is in what I call General Information Books. We've already discussed one such book, the "ROSTER AND RECORD OF IOWA SOLDIERS IN THE WAR OF THE REBELLION." Some more useful general information books on Iowa in the Civil War are:

IOWA COLONELS AND THEIR REGIMENTS. By A. A. Stuart. This book provides biographical information concerning the various colonels of Iowa regiments and some general information on what his particular regiment did.

IOWA AND THE REBELLION. By Lurton Dunham Ingersoll. This book is a general overview of the regimental histories of all the Iowa regiments. Its a guide to regimental movements, action they participated in, casualties in major activities, and maybe even contain reference too your ancestor.

ADJUTANT GENERALS RECORDS. Published by F. W. Palmer, State Printer, in Des Moines. This series of books published annually from 1861 onward is a gold mine of information about Iowans in the Civil War and Iowa's involvement in the Civil War. For the years covering the Civil War there are over 6,000 pages of information specifically on Iowa troops. A considerable amount of the records are devoted to regimental strength reports. In these pages you will find specific reference to your ancestor, maybe only a line or two, but his name will be there. Also in these reports you will find various references too camp conditions, sanitary conditions, recruiting, battle and casualty reports sent to the State Adjutant General by regimental officers, and many more subjects of interest. There is even reference in the records to some of the Iowans who enlisted in out of state regiments. Each annual volume contains a handy index. To thoroughly research your ancestor in the Adjutant Generals Records, look up regimental information for his unit for every year of the war, plus any reference from his commanding officer(s) and action he was engaged in. There is not a master index, so you will have to go to each year specifically. Using the Adjutant Generals records alone, you may be able to piece together all of the information about your ancestor that you can hope too, or want to, find out. These books van be found in either of the State Historical Society of Iowa libraries as well as some larger libraries, and university libraries.

A couple of other useful General Information Books from a national perspective are:

MILITARY BIBLIOGRAPHY OF THE CIVIL WAR. By Charles E. Dornbusch. Published in four volumes by the New York Public Library, Fifth Avenue and 42nd Street, New York, NY. 10018. Also available in some libraries. This book is considered the single most important work in print today concerning a regiments complete history. Dornbusch's work lists all printed material relating to regimental histories and also provides numerous pages of personnel narratives, memoirs and diaries. The State Historical Society of Iowa libraries have this excellent reference book also.

A COMPENDIUM OF THE WAR OF THE REBELLION. By Frederick Dyer. This book was originally published around the turn of the century in three volumes and was republished in 1959 by T. Y. Yoseloff, and is currently printed in two volumes by the Morningside Bookshop in Dayton, Ohio. Contained in Dyer's "Compendium" are Regimental histories detailing the complete movements of the regiment, the battles, engagements, skirmishes, and other service activities it engaged in; a chronology of battles, engagements, skirmishes, etc., and what regiments took part; and information on commanding officers, for the Union Army

To help use any general information book concerning the Civil War, it will be necessary to use the "ROSTER AND RECORD" or any of the previously mentioned general reference books, to determine who were the officers of the regiment and company in which your relative served. Companies had as their officers (from the top down) a captain, first lieutenant, second lieutenant, first through fifth sergeants, and corporals. At the regimental level a colonel commanded the entire regiment, followed by a lieutenant colonel, and then a major. Additionally, other staff of a regiment consisted of various surgeons, adjutants, drum majors, chaplains, and sutlers. Above the regimental level, four or more regiments were combined together into a brigade which was sometimes commanded by a brigadier general, more often by a senior colonel. Divisions were composed of two, three, or more brigades, and generally were commanded by a brigadier general. Army corps were composed of three or four (and sometimes more) divisions, and generally were commanded by a major general. Officer positions changed frequently. Some Iowa regiments had three or more colonels in their history, and numerous changes in officers of lower rank.

Officer information will also be handy in using the most comprehensive literary work of the Civil War, the massive 128 volume "OFFICIAL RECORDS OF THE UNION AND CONFEDERATE ARMIES IN THE WAR OF THE REBELLION" (OR) and its companion 31 volume "OFFICIAL RECORDS OF THE UNION AND CONFEDERATE NAVIES IN THE WAR OF THE REBELLION" (ORN). Contained in these volumes are the actual battle reports, troop movement reports, unit strength reports, casualty reports, correspondences and communications of everyone from Presidents Lincoln and Davis on down through the colonels of regiments, and sometimes even lower ranking officers. Its an awesome set of books with what appears overwhelming information, but with a little discrimination you can narrow the focus of your search down to the specific unit, sometimes even specific individual(s) you are researching. It is possible that amongst all of the written information found in these books that you will find reference to your ancestor. It is more likely that you will find numerous references to your ancestors company in the reports of colonels or generals in command of lower levels of troop organization. The OR and the ORN can be found at both State Historical Society of Iowa locations, university libraries, and a few other libraries and locations in Iowa.

Using the OR and the ORN begins with the Indexes. For both the OR and the ORN there is an entire volume which serves as a General Index. This is just the initial guide. The General Index will reference a series and a volume. Once you have located the appropriate volume(s), you must then turn to another index at the end of each volume to locate the specific page number(s) your item of research is located on. If you are researching a specific individual, you may find the person simply mentioned in an officers report. If it is officers reports you are researching or a regimental report, you will probably find scattered reports throughout the entire series of books. Also, for each volume referenced by Roman numeral there may actually be two or three separate books. The OR and the ORN are each set up so that a specific increment of the Civil War is covered in each volume. When multiple books cover a specific area, one will normally contain battle, troop movement, and regimental reports of various kinds and the other(s) will contain correspondences. Even for a given reference from the General Index (if there are two or three books in the volume number) you will have to consult the index of each book to find the information you seek.

When using the OR and the ORN you may first try looking up your ancestors name in the General Index to see if per chance there is reference to him somewhere. Be cautioned that in a war with over two million soldiers, there are many with the same name, so make sure you can verify the correct person by their affiliation. Next, try looking up references to the unit in which your ancestor served. Following that, you should try looking up references to the various commanding officers in the chain of command over your ancestor. This becomes a little more difficult considering the changes in commanding officers and changes in composition of brigades, divisions, and corps. You will find in the OR and the ORN periodical references to troop strengths and the organization of Army Corps. In these references you can find who was in charge of the various corps, divisions, brigades, and regiments, at a particular time. Using these names you can look up their reports.

The OR and the ORN contain an overwhelming amount of information, but it is very helpful information, particularly if you want to research a specific skirmish, engagement, or battle in which an ancestor may have been a participant, a casualty, or was decorated for heroism.

Some of the Iowa Regiments were fortunate enough to have individuals within their ranks who wrote books concerning their regiments history. These books are very informative and many of them contain ample reference to specific companies and references to specific individuals. Appendix B provides a listing of the regimental histories that have been written. Finding the book you want may be a problem, most have been out of print for a number of years. If they are not in your local library, try either of the State Historical Society of Iowa locations, a university library, or inter library loan. Additionally, some of the old and rare book dealer outlets may be able to assist you. One that I have dealt with that deals specifically in out of print Civil War books and reprints of Civil War regimental histories is the Camp Pope Book Shop in Iowa City. Clark Kenyon who operates the business is helpful and very knowledgable about the Civil War.

A word of caution about any of the books you may consult for reference. These books, except for reproductions, are old, rare, and often in a fragile state. **HANDLE THEM WITH CARE AND RESPECT.** If you are going to make copies of certain portions of the book, be certain you obtain permission from the owner to do so. Most of these books, except for reproductions, will be old enough that copyright is not a problem. But, the very act of making copies can cause damage to the book binding and already fragile pages. **BE CAREFUL!**

Beyond books, you have at your access thousands of writings in various periodicals which contain reference to Iowa and the Civil War. Nationally published periodicals as described in Appendix C will contain references. You can contact the publishers editorial headquarters and request reproductions of what information they have concerning your ancestors regiment. At the state level you will probably find even more information. Within the periodicals published by the State Historical Society of Iowa; THE PALIMPEST, THE ANNALS OF IOWA, THE IOWA HISTORICAL RECORD, THE IOWA

JOURNAL OF HISTORY, and the IOWA JOURNAL OF HISTORY AND POLITICS, are numerous published accounts, unit histories, Civil War diaries and letters, and dissertations about episodes of the Civil War. Most of the larger libraries and, of course, our State Historical Society libraries, contain complete volumes of these works. Your best bet is too find the master indexes for these works and look under Civil War. You may find reference to something published from a member of your ancestors unit, a key event in his units service such as a battle they participated in, or information about a commanding officer of his regiment. Master indexes for these periodicals generally cover only a specific period of time, say ten to twenty years, so there will be several master indexes you need to consult to do a thorough search.

    A very helpful reference is "IOWA IN THE CIVIL WAR: A REFERENCE GUIDE" by James J. Robertson Jr. published in the April 1961 issue of the IOWA JOURNAL OH HISTORY and also as a book by the State Historical Society of Iowa. Robertson's guide provides thorough reference to general publications about the Civil War, specific publications concerning Iowa's involvement in the Civil War, notable Iowans in the Civil War, as well as regimental history publications. Robertson lists both books and periodical literature. Robertson's guide lists references and publications published up to 1961. For periodical references about Iowa in the Civil War after 1961 consult "IOWA HISTORY AND CULTURE-A BIBLIOGRAPHY OF MATERIALS PUBLISHED BETWEEN 1962 AND 1986" pages 293-298, compiled by Patricia Dawson and David Hudson. For any periodical literature after 1986, consult annual indexes of the publication.

    On a local level, try consulting newspapers. Local newspapers contained war correspondences from members of locally recruited companies, reports of injuries and casualties of local soldiers, even reprints of letters sent home to relatives from soldiers at the front. Many of these are on microfilm and are difficult to read and research, but such a search will provide valuable insight. You will have to go through the newspapers page by page, issue by issue, to derive such information, so it is a very time consuming process, although most people who conduct such a search do find it enjoyable.

A FEW OTHER HELPFUL HINTS AND SOURCES

The Civil War is a hot topic in our country. It always has been, it always will be. The mystique, the honor, the chivalry, and all of the horrors that accompanied the war, interest nearly everyone. There's a lot of people out there who, like myself, have devoted considerable time and effort to becoming a scholar of the war, (commonly called buffs). Then, there are those who as a hobby spend their weekends and spare time taking part in reenactments of battles and other facets of Civil War soldiers' lives. Additionally, there are several Civil War Round tables in Iowa. Round tables are organized groups of people who get together regularly and hold meetings and study sessions concerning the Civil War. If you know any buffs, re-enactors, or round table members, these people can often offer up some very good insight and advice to assist you in conducting your search.

You may need to call upon the services of the Iowa Genealogical Society in order to establish the name(s) and location(s) of your long lost ancestor. For a token fee the society can conduct some searches for you, or they can provide instruction in how you can do the research yourself. The address and phone number is: Iowa Genealogical Society, P. O. Box 773, Des Moines, IA. 50322.

I have used census data records to ascertain the location of a few Civil War soldiers and the family relationships of some that I suspected of being father/son enlistees. Census records work great, but it takes some time to go through them. You need to go to your local library and have them request the records from the State Historical Society of Iowa, or you can go to either of the State Historical Society locations yourself and look up the information. Many county historical societies also have complete sets of census data records for the State of Iowa. For out of state records, consult the Iowa Genealogical society. Census records are on microfilm and are indexed by county. Within each record the listing is further broken down into townships and communities. The more precisely you can pin down the location of the individual(s) you are researching, the better. If you do not know the precise location or suspected location of an individual, you will need to search the entire county record, a very time consuming process.

Generally, the years you will be concerned with are census data records for 1850, 1860, and 1870.

Perhaps the greatest advice I can give you is that of persistency. As Jesus says in Matthew 6 vs. 7: "Ask, and it will be given you; seek, and you will find; knock, and it will be opened unto you." A researcher lives by the principle of turning stone after stone until a clue, or the information they are looking for, is discovered. Often, by association of events and the soldier in question, the researcher is able to surmise events concerning the soldier(s) in question. Of extreme value in the research process is asking questions and using the phone. Ask questions of those who may be able to help, and just get on the phone and start calling, even if you have but only a vague idea of where to start. As an inventor and researcher I have often found the phone call principle "If you can't find what you are looking for after seven calls it doesn't exist," to hold true If you get frustrated in your endeavor, or run into dead ends, just lay it aside for awhile and come back to it later. Often I have found that with time you stumble upon things or learn new things that help you in your quest.

As I stated at the beginning of this guidebook - ENJOY! Researching your Civil War ancestors past is an adventure, a thrilling adventure. As you search you live their lives, you walk in their shoes. Perhaps you will find that your ancestor was at the terrible Battle of Shiloh, maybe even one of those who saved the Union Army in the West at a location called the "Hornets Nest" on the first day of that battle. Or, maybe you will find he was detailed to one of the regiments whose duty was more mundane, such has the 9th Iowa Cavalry or the famous 37th Infantry (Greybeard Regiment). Maybe he fought indians in the Dakota's during the Civil War as did the Iowa 6th and 7th Cavalry. Or maybe you've got a real sleeper in your ancestry such as the three known Iowans who were part of the 11th Pennsylvania Cavalry Company A and were at Appomatox on April 9, 1865, the day General Lee surrendered to General Grant.

Being able to assimilate facts and link occurrences is integral to developing your ancestors story. When you have all of your information together, be certain to write the story up. That way you will have recorded your ancestors story for posterity, and some other ancestor won't have to retrace all of your steps at some other distant point in time.

ANOTHER EXAMPLE

As a further example of how you can use all of the information you have assembled, I close with a short story of the first Civil War deaths in my home town area during the Civil War. Like the opening story, it demonstrates the value of using various sources of information and the linking of facts to reconstruct events in a soldiers life. I have provided a footnote type of annotation to let the reader understand from what sources I derived my facts for this interesting little story.

FIRST REMINDERS OF A COSTLY WAR

Is it possible to fathom the trials bought upon our nation, and its citizens, when we found ourselves embroiled in the Civil War? That terrible war seems so remote in our past. It ripped our nation in two and brought on four years of unsurpassed strife. No part of what comprised the United States and its territories survived the war untouched. The greatest debt extolled was to the families whose sons and fathers never returned.

We look back on the Civil War era and ask in amazement, why did men do that? Why did men enlist and submit themselves to such agony as forced marches of over 20 miles a day in the hot sun while wearing woolen uniforms and having only scant rations to eat? If wounded in battle, they knew they may lay for days upon the field, or in a field hospital, before they would receive medical attention that at best was archaic by today's standards. If combat was not their demise, deadly diseases which reached epidemic proportions amongst the troops very well could be. In spite of such peril, men headed the call, and the principles of our great nation were sustained, but at a heavy price -- a very heavy price. With over a half million casualties, no other war in the history of the United States has exacted such a toll.

Locally, I find that Benton County received its first christening into the costs of war on November 7, 1861, when Private William Dempsey, from Vinton, who served in Company D of the Eighth Iowa

Infantry, died of "Lung Fever".[1] Six days later, George A. Holt also from Vinton, and the same company, died the same death.[2] Both men had enlisted on August 14, 1861, and mustered in on September 16, 1861.[3] They were destined to be casualties of early hardships. With minimal training, poorly equipped, and pressed hard by the demands of war in inclement fall weather, conditions were so harsh during its first few months in the field that every camp of the 8th Iowa Infantry left a graveyard.[4]

Inspired to search even closer to home, I wondered, who were the unfortunate first casualties among those who trod the same soils of my roots near Garrison? At the time of the Civil War the town did not yet exist. One community, Geneva, existed a few miles to the south, and another named Gomersal was established less than a mile further down the road.[5] A semblance of two other communities existed at Big Grove and Carlisle Grove, both also just a few miles from present day Garrison. We are reminded of Geneva today by a grove of trees and a few building foundations in a farmers field. Of Gig Grove and Carlisle Grove, only cemeteries remain. In Gomersal, a place senior citizens do not recall, and not even a building foundation exists to remind us of its presence, the Civil War's first victim of the area resided - Peter Kabrick.[6]

Peter Kabrick was a true pioneer patriot. He enlisted in Benton Counties first company mustered for the war, Company G of the 5th Iowa Infantry.[7] An irony of Kabrick's enlistment is that his state of nativity; Virginia, was soundly for the Confederacy. Kabrick and his company left Vinton amongst much fanfare on July 9, 1861. The 5th Iowa was mustered in at Camp Warren near Burlington where they, like the 8th Iowa Infantry, received only a few weeks of instruction before being sent to Keokuk on August 2, 1861.[8] Iowa was threatened at this time by Martin Henry Green's Confederate forces.

---

[1] HISTORY OF BENTON COUNTY IOWA, (1910): VOLUME 1.
[2] Ibid.
[3] Ibid.
[4] IOWA AND THE REBELLION.
[5] THE HISTORY OF BENTON COUNTY, IOWA- 1988.
[6] ROSTER AND RECORD OF IOWA SOLDIERS IN THE REBELLION: VOLUME1.
[7] HISTORY OF BENTON COUNTY (1910): VOLUME 1.
[8] IOWA AND THE REBELLION.

Green had recruited a Confederate Cavalry in Northern Missouri which may have, in fact probably did have, Iowans amongst its ranks. Green and his cavalry were intent upon attacking Keokuk. When the 5th Iowa was in the Keokuk area, the Battle of Athens (actually only a glorified skirmish) occurred just a across the border in Missouri.[9] A combination of Union and home guard forces successfully chased Green and his entourage off. During this exchange a few rebel cannon shells and musket shot were fired across the Des Moines River onto Iowa, making the Battle of Athens the only Civil War combat to occur on Iowa soil.

Following the Keokuk excursion, the 5th Iowa Infantry was involved in various movements in Missouri until the spring of 1862 when it became involved in more serious action.[10] Peter Kabrick would have no part of it. After all the tramping around Missouri the 5th Iowa had done, fatigue and camp plague caught up with him. On February 7, 1862, records show Kabrick as sick and in the hospital.[11] A Certificate of Undertakers of the U. S. Military Hospitals states that the 26 year old died on April 2, 1862 of Small Pox at the St. Louis Small Pox Hospital. His effects were burned and his regiment was not even notified of his death until November.[12] When his family was notified is unknown. He is memorialized at Big Grove Cemetery as dying April 20, 1862, an error of the record keeping and communication systems of the time.

Four days following Peter Kabrick's death the first battle fatality of the area occurred.[13] Once again, Gomersal was the unlucky recipient of such distinction. Samuel C. Martin had become a member of the Benton County Guards. At least half the members of the Guards came from the Garrison Area.[14] They left for camp on October 15, 1861 and became the 13th Iowa Infantry Company G.[15] One member of the company, Buren R. Sherman a prominent attorney from Vinton, would later serve as Governor of Iowa. At their camp of

---

[9] A COMPENDIUM OF THE WAR OF THE REBELLION.
[10] IOWA AND THE REBELLION.
[11] NATIONAL ARCHIVE MILITARY RECORDS.
[12] NATIONAL ARCHIVE MILITARY RECORDS.
[13] HISTORY OF BENTON COUNTY IOWA. (1910): VOLUME 1.
[14] HISTORY OF BENTON COUNTY IOWA, (1910): VOLUME 1.
[15] IOWA AND THE REBELLION.

instruction, Camp McClellan near Davenport, the 13th Iowa Infantry received merciless drilling for hours on end. Their Colonel, Marcellus M. Crocker, was a stern disciplinarian.[16] So much so that he caused intense consternation among the men. Crocker would later be promoted to Brigadier General.[17]

The 13th Iowa's first detail was guard duty from December 1861 to March 1862 at Jefferson City, Missouri.[18] From there the Regiment was moved to Pittsburg Landing where on that fateful day of April 6, 1861 it became involved in Iowa's great battle of the rebellion - Shiloh.[19] As Iowa troops were beginning to arouse that Sunday morning, Confederate forces pulled a sneak attack. A long roll of the drum summoned the 13th Iowa Infantry and into battle the green troops who had never even skirmished were hurled. In spite of its inexperience, the regiment fought with great efficiency. Crockers stern discipline had paid off, and another complaint was never heard from members of the 13th about their demanding Colonel.[20] Colonel Abraham M. Hare of the 11th Iowa Infantry commanded the First Brigade of the First Division of the Army of the Tennessee, then under command of General U. S. Grant, of which the 13th Iowa Infantry was a part. In excerpts from his report of Shiloh Hare mentioned:[21]

"....Early in the morning of the 6th, upon the alarm being given, the brigade composed of the Eighth and Eighteenth Regiments Illinois Infantry, and Eleventh and Thirteenth Regiments Iowa Infantry, and Dresser's battery, were formed in the open field in front of their respective encampments. I received orders about 8 o'clock a. m. to move three regiments to the left of the Second Brigade. The Eighth and Eighteenth Illinois and Thirteenth Iowa were accordingly ordered....After seeing the order executed I joined the regiments at their position....I found

---

[16] IOWA AND THE REBELLION.
[17] IOWA COLONELS AND THEIR REGIMENTS.
[18] A COMPENDIUM OF THE WAR OF THE REBELLION.
[19] IOWA AND THE REBELLION.
[20] IOWA COLONELS AND THEIR REGIMENTS.
[21] OFFICIAL RECORDS OF THE UNION AND CONFEDERATE ARMIES IN THE WAR OF THE REBELLION. SERIES I, VOLUME 10, PART I, REPORTS.

this position of my brigade there formed under the fire of the enemies cannon and musketry....A charge being made by these bodies of the enemy's infantry, directed upon the battery and our infantry on the right, they broke and retired in great disorder....

Having retired to the distance of about 100 yards I succeeded, with the assistance of the field officers of my regiments, in rallying them and forming them in line in the same order as before. Here we maintained our position in good order, under a constant fire of the enemy, until 12 o'clock m., when discovering the enemy were approaching in great numbers....I ordered my regiments to retire and take up a new position about 200 yards to the rear, which we did in good order and without confusion. We remained in this position, repelling charge after charge of the enemy, until 4:30 o'clock p. m., all officers and men behaving with the greatest gallantry. At that hour, my regiments having exhausted their ammunition and great numbers of them having been killed and wounded....I again ordered them to fall back, which was done in good order as before....

To Col. M. M. Crocker of the Thirteenth Iowa Volunteers, I wish to call special attention. The coolness and bravery displayed by him on the field of battle during the entire action of the 6th, the skill with which he maneuvered his men, and the example of daring and disregard to danger by which he inspired them to do their duty and stand by their colors, show him to be possessed of the highest qualities of a commander...."

Colonel Crocker in his report of the battle stated:[22]

"....Early in the morning of the 6th the alarm was given, and heavy firing in the distance indicated that our camp was attacked. The regiment was formed in front of its color line, its full force consisting of 717 men, rank and file. It was at once ordered to

---

[22] OFFICIAL RECORDS OF THE UNION AND CONFEDERATE ARMIES IN THE WAR OF THE REBELLION. SERIES I, VOLUME 10, PART I, REPORTS.

form on the left of the Second Brigade, and proceeded to that position at a double-quick, and was then formed in line of battle in a skirt of woods bordering on an open field to the left of a battery. Here it remained for some time inactive, while the enemy's guns were playing on our battery. In the mean time a large force of the enemy's infantry were filing around the open field in front of our line, protected by the woods and in the direction of our battery, opening a heavy fire of musketry on the infantry stationed on our right and charging upon the battery. The infantry and the battery on the right having given way, and the enemy advancing at double-quick, we gave them one round of musketry and also gave way....Having retired to the distance of 200 yards we succeeded in rallying and forming a good line....and having fronted to the enemy, held our position there under a continual fire of cannon and musketry until after 12 o'clock, when we were ordered to retire and take up a new position....Here, having formed a new line, we maintained it under incessant fire until 4:30 o'clock p.m., the men conducting themselves with great gallantry and coolness, and doing great execution on the enemy, repulsing charge after charge, and driving them back with great loss...."

The Thirteenth Iowa Infantry on that first day of the Battle of Shiloh was in the front line of battle for 10 hours and suffered 172 casualties of which 24 were deaths.[23] Company G suffered 10 wounded and 1 death; Samuel C. Martin, killed by a musket ball to the head, bringing death instantly.[24] The 23 year old private, a plasterer by trade, left a wife Mary.[25]

In researching Samuel Martin's death, a couple of interesting twists came to light. In Company G's roster, another Martin, Charles M., is also listed.[26] They both enlisted on September 27, 1861, and

---

[23] IOWA AND THE REBELLION.
[24] NATIONAL ARCHIVE PENSION RECORDS.
[25] NATIONAL ARCHIVE PENSION RECORDS.
[26] ROSTER AND RECORD OF IOWA SOLDIERS IN THE WAR OF THE REBELLION: VOLUME 2.

mustered in October 28, 1861.[27] And, the nativity of both is listed as Ohio. Charles M. rose to the rank of First Sergeant and died of chronic diarrhoea on June 7, 1864.[28] Could there be a relationship between the Samuel and Charles? Brothers perhaps? Charles M. is buried beside his parents Robert and Phoebe in the Big Grove Cemetery. Checking obituaries of both his parents in the Vinton Eagle yielded no clue to a relationship.[29] In the Martin family biography in the 1910 "History of Benton County, Iowa," an answer is found.[30] Robert and Phoebe had nine children, two of whom did not survive to adulthood, but none by the name of Samuel. If there was a relationship between Samuel and Charles, such as perhaps first cousins, only genealogical records from the state of Ohio could clarify.

Samuel Martin's widow, Mary, when she applied for a veteran widows pension, was required to have two witnesses from Gomersal state in writing that she was indeed the widow of Samuel Martin.[31] This was probably due to the noted cases of fraud which occurred in the pension system. Signing the document were Tomizin Culp and Francis M. Flickinger. Mary was granted a widows pension of $8.00/month in January 1863.[32] While meandering the Big Grove Cemetery researching Civil War veterans I found a small head stone perched at the highest point of the cemetery. On one side of the stone is etched a memorial epitaph to Francis M. Flickinger, age 19, who died at Helena Arkansas on February 27, 1863. On another side is etched a memorial epitaph to Tomizin Culp, age 22, who was killed at the Battle of Cedar Creek on October 19, 1864. Both men were in the 28th Iowa Infantry Company A, another locally raised company.[33] On another side of the stone I find that Culp's 22 year old wife, Susan, had died four months before him.

These are all nearly forgotten people who traveled the roads of a nearly forgotten community over 130 years ago. They were a people of principle in a war torn country. They paid a heavy price to

---

[27] ROSTER AND RECORD OF IOWA SOLDIERS IN THE WAR OF THE REBELLION: VOLUME 2.
[28] ROSTER AND RECORD OF IOWA SOLDIERS IN THE WAR OF THE REBELLION: VOLUME 2.
[29] VINTON EAGLE NEWSPAPERS OF 1882 AND 1887.
[30] HISTORY OF BENTON COUNTY, IOWA (1910): VOLUME 2.
[31] NATIONAL ARCHIVE PENSION RECORDS.
[32] NATIONAL ARCHIVE PENSION RECORDS.
[33] HISTORY OF BENTON COUNTY IOWA, (1910): VOLUME 1.

maintain their principles and their country. The less we know of, or recall, the tumultuous time of the Civil War, the easier it becomes to allow the same conditions which gave rise to our countries Civil War to happen again. Those who study history know that unless its lessons are taken to heart, it repeats itself. The departed heroes who fought and died for our countries priciples, I'm sure would rather we never face such perils again.

APPENDIX A

ADDRESSES OF STATE HISTORICAL INSTITUTIONS

ALABAMA: State of Alabama Department of Archives and History, 624 Washington Avenue, Montgomery, AL. 36130.

ARKANSAS: Arkansas History Commission, One Capitol Mall, Little Rock, AR. 72201.

CALIFORNIA: California State Archives, 1020 O Street, Room 130, Sacramento, CA. 95814.

COLORADO: Division of State Archives and Public Records, 1313 Sherman Street, Denver, CO. 80203.

CONNECTICUT: The Adjutant General Attention: Records Officer, State Armory, 360 Broad Street, Hartford, CT. 06115. Or: Connecticut State Library, 231 Capitol Avenue, Hartford, CT. 06115.

DELAWARE: Bureau of Archives-Modern Records, Hall of Records, Dover, DE. 19901.

FLORIDA: Florida State Archives, Department of State, R.A. Gray Building, Tallahassee, FL. 32301.

GEORGIA: Georgia Department of Archives and History, Civil War Records Section, 330 Capital Avenue SW, Atlanta, GA. 30334.

ILLINOIS: The Director Archives-Records Management Division, Office of the Secretary of State, Springfield, IL. 62756.

INDIANA: Archives and Records Management Division, Military Records, Indiana Commission of Public Records, 140 North Senate Avenue, Indianpolis, IN 46204

IOWA: State Historical Society of Iowa, Capitol Complex, Des Moines, IA. 50319. And, State Historical Society of Iowa, 402 Iowa Avenue, Iowa City, IA. 52240.

KANSAS: Kansas State Historical Society, Dept. of Archives, Center for Historical Research, 120 West 10th Street Topeka, KS. 66612.

KENTUCKY: Kentucky Historical Society, Old State House, PO Box H, Frankfurt, KY. 40601.

LOUISIANA: State of Louisiana, Secretary of State, Division of Archives, Records Management and History, PO Box 94125, Baton Rouge, LA. 70804-9125.

MAINE: State of Maine, Maine State Archives, L-H-A Building, State House Sation 84, Augusta, ME. 04333.

MARYLAND: State Archives, 350 Rowe Boulevard, Annapolis, MD. 21401.

MASSACHUSETTS: The Commonwealth of Massachusetts Military Division, The Adjutant General's Office, Military Records Section, Room 1000, 100 Cambridge Street, Boston, MA. 02201.

MICHIGAN: Michigan Department of State Bureau of History, State Archives, 3405 North Logan Street, Lansing, MI. 48918.

MINNESOTA: Division of Library and Archives, Minnesota Historical Society, 1500 Mississippi Street, St. Paul, MN. 55101.

MISSISSIPPI: Archives and Library Division, PO Box 571, Jackson, MS. 39205.

MISSOURI: Adjutant's General Office, 1717 Industrial Drive, Jefferson City, MO. 65101.

NEVADA: Nevada State Library and Archives, Division of Archives and Records, 101 South Fall Street, Carson City, NV. 89710.

NEW HAMPSHIRE: Division of Records and Archives, 71 South Fruit Street, Concord, NH. 03301.

NEW JERSEY: Department of State Division of Archives, nd Records Management, Archives Section, 185 West State Street, Cn 307, Trenton, NJ. 08625.

NEW MEXICO: State Records Center and Archives, 404 Montezuma, Sante Fe, NM. 87503.

NEW YORK: New York State Archives, Room 11D40, Cultural Education Center, Empire State Plaza, Albany, NY. 12230.

NORTH CAROLINA: Division of Archives and History, Dept. of Cultural Resources, 109 E Jones Street, Raleigh, NC. 27611.

OHIO: Ohio State Archives Library, 1985 Velma Avenue, Columbus, OH. 43211.

OKLAHOMA: Division of Library Resources, Oklahoma Historical Society, Historical Building, Oklahoma City, OK. 73105.

PENNSYLVANIA: Director, Pennsylvania Historical and Museum Commission, Archives Building, Box 1026, Harrisburg, PA. 17108-1026.

RHODE ISLAND: Rhode Island Civil War Archives, Benefit Street Arsenal, 176 Benefit Street, Providence, RI. 02903.

SOUTH CAROLINA: South Carolina Dept. of Archives and History, PO Box 11, 669 Capitol Station, Columbia, SC. 29211.

SOUTH DAKOTA: Historical Resources Center Memorial Building, Pierre, SD. 57501.

TENNESSEE: Public Service Section, Tennessee State Library and Archives, 403 7th Avenue North, Nashville, TN. 37219-5041.

TEXAS: Texas State Library, Archives Division, PO Box 12927, Austin, TX. 78711.

VERMONT: State Veterans Affairs, State Office Building, Montpelier, VT. 05602.

VIRGINIA: Archives Division, Virginia State Library, 11th and Capitol Streets, Richmond, VA. 23219.

WEST VIRGINIA: West Virginia Department of Culture and History, Division of Archives and History, The Cultural Center, Capitol Complex, Charleston, WV. 25305.

WISCONSIN: Reference Archivist, The State Historical Society of Wisconsin, 816 State Street, Madison, WI. 53706.

APPENDIX B

IOWA CIVIL WAR REGIMENTAL HISTORY BOOKS

NOTE A ____ indicates no recognized author.

1st Iowa Infantry

Ware, Eugene F. The Lyon Campaign in Missouri. Topeka, KS. Crane & Co, 1907. 377p.

Wilkie, Franc B. Pen and Powder. Boston. Ticknor, 1888. 383p.

2nd Iowa Infantry

Cate, Wirt Armistead, ed. Two Soldiers: The Campaign Diaries of Thomas J. Key, C.S.A., December 7, 1863-May 17, 1865, and Robert J. Campbell, U.S.A., January 1, 1864-July 21, 1864. Chapel Hill, NC. Univ. of NC. Press, 1938. 277p.

Twombly, Voltaire P. The Second Iowa Infantry at Fort Donelson, February 15, 1862, Together with an Outline History of the Regiment from its Organization at Keokuk, IA, May 27, 1861, to Final Discharge at Davenport, Iowa, July 20, 1865. Des Moines, IA. Plain Talking Printing House, 1897. 27 p.

3rd Iowa Infantry

Thompson, Seymour D. Recollections with the Third Iowa Regiment. Cincinnati, OH. 1864. 396 p.

4th Iowa Infantry

Ankeny, Henry G. Kiss Josey for Me!. Santa Ana, CA. Friis-Pioneer Press, 1974. 250 p.

5th Iowa Infantry

_____ What I Saw in Dixie: Or, Sixteen Months in Rebel Prisons. Dansville, NY. Robbins & Poore, 1868. 126 p.

_____ With Fire and Sword. NY. Neale, 1911. 203 p.

6th Iowa Infantry

Wright, Henry. A History of the Sixth Iowa Infantry. Iowa City, IA. State Hist. Soc., 1923. 539 p.

7th Iowa Infantry

Smith, Henry I. History of the Seventh Iowa Veteran Volunteer Infantry During the Civil War. Mason City, IA. E. Hitchcock, 1903. 313 p.

11th Iowa Infantry

Fultz, William S. War Reminiscences: History of Company "D" Eleventh Regiment, Iowa Volunteers. Wilton, IA. 1885. 72 p.

12th Iowa Infantry

Clark, Charles B., and Bowen, Roger B. University Recruits: Company C, 12th Iowa Infantry Regiment U.S.A. 1861-1866. Elverson, PA. Mennonite Family Hist, 1989. 439 p.

Reed, David W. Campaigns and Battles of the Twelfth Regiment Iowa Veteran Volunteer Infantry, from Organization, September, 1861, to Muster-Out, January 20, 1866. Evanston, IL. 1903. 319 p.

Rich, Joseph W. The Battle of Shiloh. Iowa City, IA. State Historical Society, 1911. 134 p.

15th Iowa Infantry

Belknap, William W. History of the Fifteenth Regiment, Iowa Veteran Volunteer Infantry, from October, 1861, to August, 1865, When Disbanded at the End of the War. Keokuk, IA. R.B. Ogden, 1887. 664 p.

Boyd, Cyrus F. The Civil War Diary of the Fifteenth Iowa Infantry, 1861-1863. Millwood, NY. Kraus, 1977. 135 p.

19th Iowa Infantry

Tilley, Nannie M., ed. Federals on the Frontier: The Diary of Benjamin F. McIntyre, 1862-1864. Austin, TX. University of Texas Press, 1963. 429 p.

20th Iowa Infantry

Barnes, J.D. What I Saw You Do: A Brief History of the Battles, Marches, and Sieges of the Twentieth Iowa Volunteer Infantry, During Their Three Years of Active Service in the War of the Rebellion. Port Byron, IL. Owen and Hall, 1896. 48 p.

Barney, Chester. Recollections of Field Service with the Twentieth Iowa Infantry Volunteers: Or, What I Saw in the Army.... Davenport, IA. Gazette Job Rooms, 1896. 323 p.

21st Iowa Infantry

Crooke, George, comp. The Twenty-first Regiment of Iowa Volunteer Infantry: A Narrative of Its Experience in Active Service, Including a Military Record of Each Officer, Non-commissioned Officer, and Private Soldier of the Organization. Milwaukee, WI. King, Fowle, 1891. 232 p.

22nd Iowa Infantry

Jones, Samuel C. Reminiscences of the Twenty-second Iowa Volunteer Infantry, Giving Its Organization, Marches, Skirmishes, Battles, and Sieges, as Taken from the Diary of Lieutenant S.C. Jones of Company A. Iowa City, IA. 1907. 164 p.

28th Iowa Infantry

Blake, Ephraim E. A Succinct History of the 28th Iowa Volunteer Infantry: From Date of Muster Into Service.to its Final Muster Out. Belle Plaine, IA. Union Press, 1896. 143 p.

32nd Iowa Infantry

Scott, John. Story of the Thirty Second Iowa Infantry Volunteers. Nevada, IA. 1896. 526 p.

33rd Iowa Infantry

Sperry, Andrew F. History of the 33d Iowa Infantry Volunteer Regiment, 1863-6. Des Moines, IA. Mills, 1866. 237 p.

34th Iowa Infantry

Clark, James S. The Thirty-fourth Iowa Regiment Brief History. Des Moines, IA. Watters-Talbott, 1892. 59 p.

35th Iowa Infantry

_____ First and Second Reunions of the Thirty-fifth Iowa Infantry Held at Muscatine, Iowa. Muscatine, IA. Journal Printing Co., 1889-1890. 57 p.

1st Iowa Cavalry

Lothrup, Charles H. <u>A History of the First Regiment Iowa Cavalry Veteran Volunteers, from its Organization in 1861 to its Muster Out of the United States Service in 1866</u>. Lyons, IA. Beers & Eaton, 1890. 422 p.

2nd Iowa Cavalry

Pierce, Lyman B. <u>History of the Second Iowa Cavalry, Containing a Detailed Account of its Organization, Marches, and the Battles in Which it has Participated; Also, a Complete Roster of Each Company</u>. Burlington, VA. Hawk-Eye Print, 1865. 237 p.

4th Iowa Cavalry

Davis, Kathleen, ed. <u>Such are the Trials: The Civil War Diaries of Jacob Gantz</u>. Ames, IA. Iowa State University Press, 1991. 122 p.

_____ <u>The Story of a Cavalry Regiment: The Career of the Fourth Iowa Veteral Volunteers from Kansas to Georgia, 1861-1865</u>. NY. Putnam's, 1893. 602 p.

6th Iowa Cavalry

Drips, Joseph. <u>Three Years Among the Indians in Dakota</u>. Kimball, SD. Brule Index, 1894. 139 p.

Myers, Frank. <u>Soldiering in Dakota, Among the Indians, in 1863-4-5</u>. Freeport, NY. Books for Libraries Press, 1971. 48 p.

7th Iowa Cavalry

Ware, Eugene F. <u>The Indian War of 1864</u>. NY. St. Martin's, 1960. 483 p.

1st Iowa Light Artillery Battery

Black, Samuel. _A Soldier's Recollections of the Civil War_. Minco, OK. Minco Minstrel, 1912. 117 p.

2nd Iowa Light Artillery Battery

Phillips, L.F. _Some Things Our Boy Saw In The War_. Gravity, IA. 1911.

APPENDIX C

CIVIL WAR MAGAZINES AND JOURNALS

AMERICA'S CIVIL WAR MAGAZINE, Empire Press, 602 E. King St., Suite 300, Leesburg, VA. 22075.

BLUE AND GRAY MAGAZINE, Blue and Gray Enterprises, Inc., P.O. Box 28685, Columbus, OH. 43228.

CIVIL WAR, The Magazine of the Civil War Society, Cool Springs Associates, P.O.Box 770, Berryville, VA. 22611.

CIVIL WAR TIMES ILLUSTRATED, Morningside House, Inc., P.O. Box 1087, Dayton, OH. 45401.

MILITARY HISTORY, Empire Press, 602 E. King Street, Leesburg, VA. 22075.

MORNINGSIDE NOTES, Morningside House, Inc., P.O. Box 1087, Dayton, OH. 45401.

CIVIL WAR ANCESTOR NOTES

ANCESTOR NAME:

DATE OF BIRTH:
    Source of information:

PLACE OF BIRTH:
    Source of information:

DATE OF DEATH:
    Source of information:

PLACE OF DEATH:
    Source of information:

REGIMENT AND COMPANY:
    Source of information:

ENLISTMENT AND MUSTER IN DATES:
    Source of information:

MUSTER OUT, DEATH, OR DISCHARGE DATE:
    Source of information:

PROMOTIONS AND OFFICES HELD:

    Source of information:

BATTLES AND SIGNIFICANT EVENTS:

    Source of information:

CIVIL WAR ANCESTOR NOTES

ANCESTOR NAME:

DATE OF BIRTH:
    Source of information:

PLACE OF BIRTH:
    Source of information:

DATE OF DEATH:
    Source of information:

PLACE OF DEATH:
    Source of information:

REGIMENT AND COMPANY:
    Source of information:

ENLISTMENT AND MUSTER IN DATES:
    Source of information:

MUSTER OUT, DEATH, OR DISCHARGE DATE:
    Source of information:

PROMOTIONS AND OFFICES HELD:

    Source of information:

BATTLES AND SIGNIFICANT EVENTS:

    Source of information:

NOTES

ABOUT THE AUTHOR

Steve Meyer is a fire service professional and free lance writer/photographer who lives in Garrison, Iowa. He is currently working on a series of books about Iowa in the Civil War. He also conducts research on Civil War veterans and Civil War events for interested people. Contact the author at the address or phone number below for information on his other Civil War writings, or for research inquiries.

WANTED:

Copies of primary information written by Iowa Civil War soldiers; diaries, letters, war correspondence, etc. Of particular interest is material from Iowans who served in the Army of the Potomac, Iowans who served in the Confederacy, and photographs of Iowa Civil War soldiers. I do not want the original documents, only copies for research and writing purposes. Direct all information on such data too; Author Steve Meyer, Box 247, Garrison, IA. 52229. ph. 319-477-5041

OTHER CIVIL WAR BOOKS BY STEVE MEYER

"IOWANS CALLED TO VALOR." A quick reading book full of facts about Iowa's entry into the Civil War. Included in the book are numerous citations from diaries and letters of Iowa Civil War soldiers which reveal their soldierly experiences in camp and as they answered the Union's call. This book is chock full of little quips and anecdotes that anyone interested in Iowa history or the Civil War would enjoy. $12.95 postpaid (Iowa residents $13.60 which includes 5% state sales tax) order from Meyer Publishing, Box 247, Garrison, IA. 52229